Life Is Like the Wind

For Riley and his mom
— Shona Innes

For Ficánka
— Írisz Agócs

First North American edition published in 2014 by Barron's Educational Series, Inc.

Text copyright © Shona Innes, 2014
Illustrations copyright © Írisz Agócs, 2014
Copyright © The Five Mile Press, 2014

All inquiries should be addressed to:
Barron's Educational Series, Inc.
250 Wireless Boulevard
Hauppauge, New York 11788
www.barronseduc.com

ISBN: 978-0-7641-6747-8
Library of Congress Control Number: 2014932021

Date of manufacture: May 2014
Manufactured by: Waiman Book Binding (China) Ltd, Kowloon, Hong Kong, China

Printed in China

9 8 7 6 5 4 3 2 1

Life Is Like the Wind

Shona Innes * Írisz Agócs

BARRON'S

Life is a precious and funny thing.

When a body is alive, it is filled with life.

We can't see life in the body, but we know when life is there.

Life makes the body move,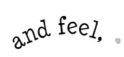

and feel,

and be with us.

Life is a little bit like the wind.
We can't see the wind, but we know when the wind is there.

The wind makes leaves flutter,
and fur fly,
and kites soar high in the sky.

When the wind goes, things are very still.
They don't flutter or blow or fly or soar anymore.

Where does the wind go when we
can't see it moving things?
It goes somewhere else.

Life is like the wind.
When life goes, the body is very still.

The body cannot move or feel
or do anything anymore.
Where does life go when it leaves the body?

People have different ideas about where a life goes when it leaves the body.
Some believe the life enters another body, to give life to a new creature.

Others believe the life goes to a happy place called heaven, where the life can enjoy its favorite things.

Some think the life goes deep into the ground,
giving new life to trees and flowers...

...or that the life goes way up into the stars,
where it twinkles brightly
and watches over us.

And some believe that a little bit of the life stays behind.

Even when the body is gone,

people remember and feel the life, still loving the life deep inside their hearts.

When the life goes from a body,
we can feel very sad.

We may miss the life very much.
But there are things we can do to feel better.

Some people say prayers and talk to the life.

Others like to collect memories of
the life to help them remember.

Some people like to spend time being kind to others.

It makes them feel better to help others have good and happy lives.

And other people just like to spend quiet time alone ...
thinking about how precious life is.

Life is very precious.
We can look after our own life by eating well, taking care of our body, and doing happy things.

We can help others look after their lives, too,
by being caring and kind to them.

A happy and loved life will stay with
a body as long as it possibly can.

But when it is time for the life to leave, it will go.

Those left behind might be very sad.

But, like the wind,
        the life must leave.

It will go somewhere else.

A note to parents and teachers from Shona:

The death of someone or something precious to a child can be difficult, even more so when, as well as losing a loved one, the child also knows that the people around them are very upset. In times of trouble, children look to others for ways to cope.

When things are difficult to explain, or cause unpleasant emotions, some adults might try to avoid conversations about the upset, leaving a child without a framework to understand or to know what to do with their feelings or the expected way to behave. *Life Is Like the Wind* was developed to provide a framework to assist with the conversations that children may need about grief.

Children, and those with some disabilities, are very concrete in their understanding. They know about what they can see, hear, touch, and feel. Explanations need to be basic, visual, explainable, and touchable.

Multiple questions can sometimes be the way a child makes sense of loss, and also a way that the child stays connected to the people close to them. Children need answers to their questions. *Life Is Like the Wind* may assist in providing some simple, helpful responses to emotive questions.

Children, like the adults around them, react differently at times of loss. There are no "right" ways to grieve. Expectations and timelines can complicate reactions. If a child is showing persistent changes in their behavior and demeanor in the weeks after everyone else in the family has settled, seek out a professional opinion — your general practitioner is often the best place to start.